Our Amazing Solar System

EARTH

Kerri Mazzarella

A Stingray Book

SEAHORSE PUBLISHING

Teaching Tips for Caregivers:

This Hi-Lo book features high-interest subject matter that will appeal to all readers in intermediate and middle school grades. It may be enjoyed by students reading at or above grade level as well as by those who are looking for age-appropriate themes matched with a less challenging reading level. Hi-Lo books are ideal for ELL readers, too.

Each book appeals to a striving reader's age and maturity level. Opportunities are provided for students to read words they already know while encountering a limited number of new, high-interest vocabulary words. With these supports in place, students will read more fluently while increasing reading comprehension. Use the following suggestions to help students grow as readers.

- Encourage the student to read independently at home.
- Encourage the student to practice reading aloud.
- Encourage activities that require reading.
- Establish a regular reading time.
- Have the student write questions about what they read.

Teaching Tips for Teachers:

Research shows that one of the best ways for students to learn a new topic is to read about it.

Before Reading

- Ask, "What do I know about this topic?"
- Ask, "What do I want to learn about this topic?"

During Reading

- Ask, "What is the author trying to teach me?"
- Ask, "How is this like something I already know?"

After Reading

- Discuss how the text features (headings, index, etc.) help with understanding the topic.
- Ask, "What interesting or fun fact did you learn?"

Table of Contents

Water, Water Everywhere 4

Home Sweet Home 6

Sunshine 8

Our Neighbors 10

Moonwalking 12

Spin, Baby, Spin 14

Our Protection 16

Digging Deep 18

Keep Learning 20

Glossary 22

Index 23

After Reading Questions 23

About the Author 24

Water, Water Everywhere

Earth may be the most unique **planet** in the universe.

It is the only planet we know that has liquid water on it. And it has a lot of water!

Did you know that 70 percent of Earth is covered in water? About 97 percent is salt water and three percent is fresh water.

Earth is sometimes called the blue planet because all its water makes it look blue from space.

Home Sweet Home

Earth is part of the Milky Way **galaxy**.

As far as we know, Earth is the only planet that has life.

Earth is home to billions of people and millions of types of plants and animals.

It is also the planet we call home.

Sunshine

The Sun is the star at the center of our **solar system**, and it is very important.

Heat and light come from the Sun. Without it, there would be no life on Earth.

Eight planets and many smaller objects **orbit** around the Sun.

Earth is the third planet away from the Sun.

There are about 90 million miles (145 million kilometers) between Earth and the Sun. It is the perfect distance. Not too hot and not too cold!

Our Neighbors

Mercury, Venus, Earth, and Mars are closest to the Sun. They are called **terrestrial** planets. They are round, small, and rocky.

Jupiter, Saturn, Uranus, and Neptune are farther away from the Sun. They are much bigger and made of mostly gas.

Sun

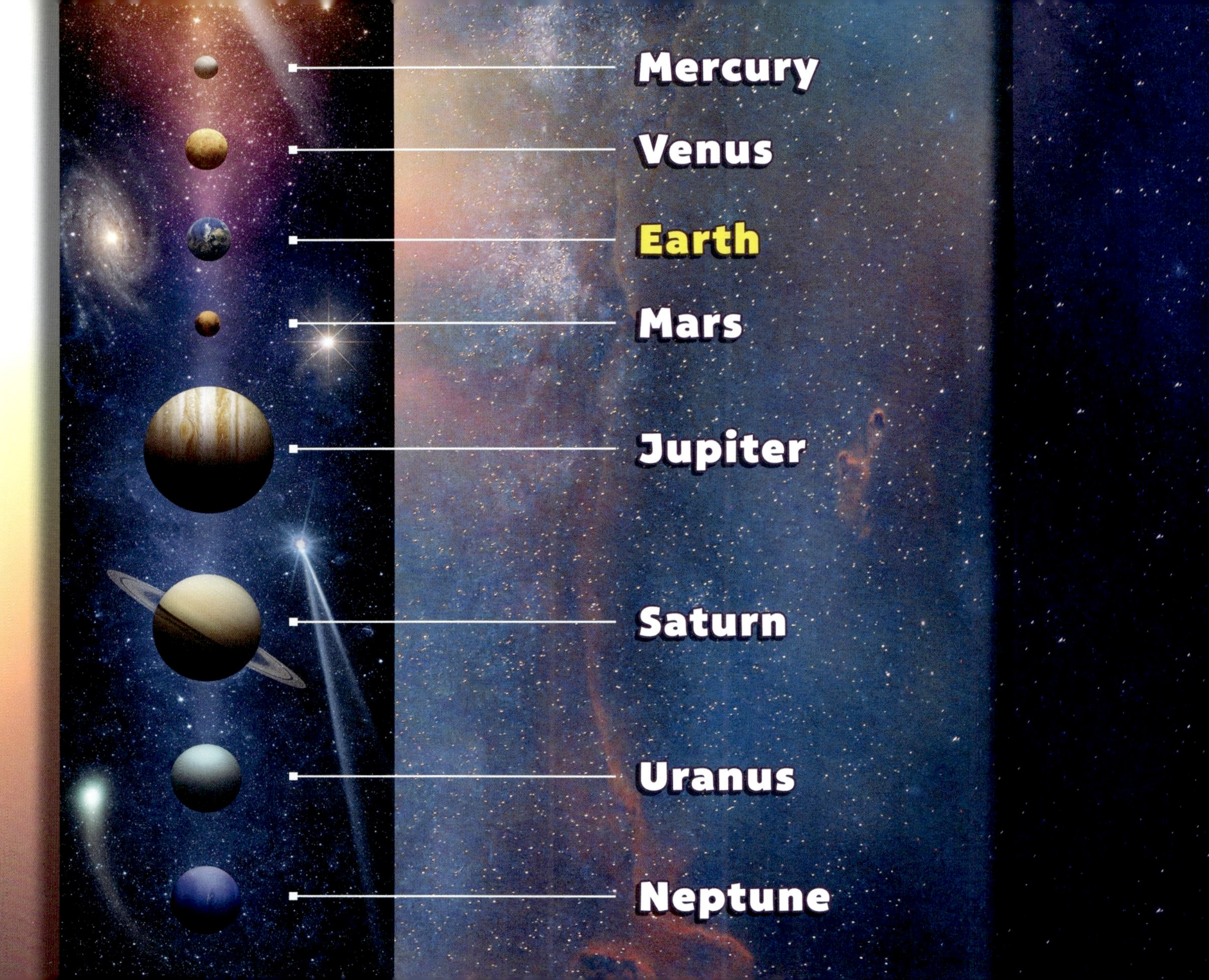
Mercury
Venus
Earth
Mars
Jupiter
Saturn
Uranus
Neptune

Moonwalking

Earth is the only planet in our solar system to have just one **moon**.

The moon does not give off its own light. It reflects light from the Sun.

On July 20, 1969, American **astronauts** walked on the moon for the first time. Their mission was called *Apollo 11*.

Spin, Baby, Spin

It takes Earth about 365 days or one year to orbit once around the Sun.

Earth also spins on its **axis** at the same time it orbits the Sun.

It takes 24 hours or one day to make a complete rotation on its axis.

One day is added to the month of February every four years to keep our calendar current. This is called a leap year.

Earth does not spin straight up and down. Its axis is tilted. Seasons are determined by which region is closer or farther away from the Sun.

Our Protection

Earth's **atmosphere** is a thick layer of gases. It is the air we breathe.

The atmosphere covers Earth and acts as a blanket to keep it warm.

It also protects us from the Sun's harmful radiation and from meteors that come from space.

The ozone layer is part of our atmosphere. It protects life from harmful ultraviolet rays that come from the Sun.

Digging Deep

Earth is made up of three layers.

The crust is a thin layer on the surface of Earth where plants, animals, and people live.

The mantle is molten rock. It is the thickest layer of Earth.

The core is the center of Earth. It is made up of extremely hot metals.

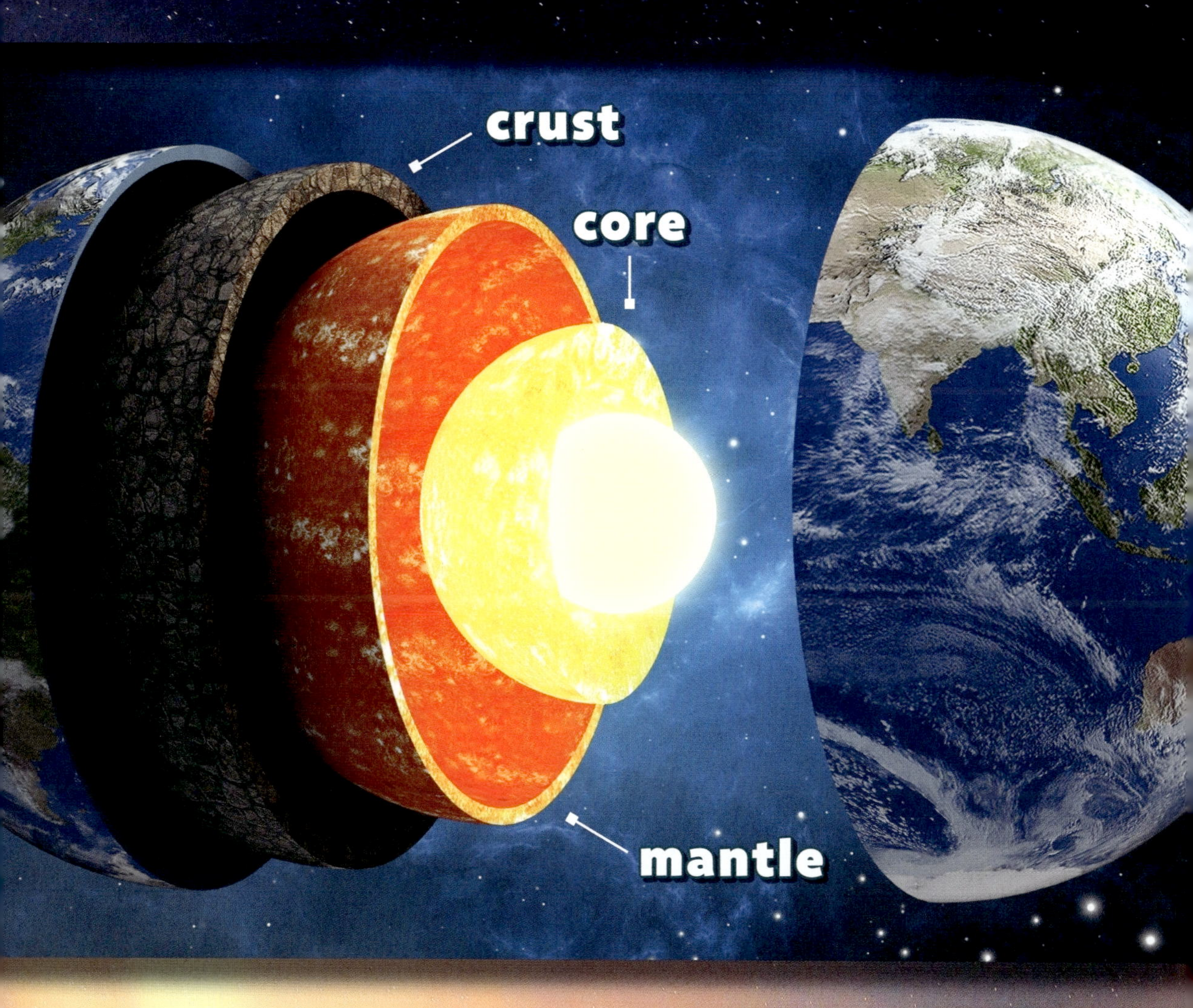

Even though the crust is the thinnest layer of Earth, it is still too thick for anyone to dig through to the next layer!

Keep Learning

Every day, scientists learn more about planet Earth and how it relates to our solar system.

They use **satellites** to gather data from space, observe planets, and provide communication.

Satellites also provide valuable information about Earth's oceans, land, and air.

Glossary

astronauts (AS-truh-nawts): people who travel in a spacecraft

atmosphere (AT-muhs-feer): the mixture of gases that surrounds a planet; all the air between the surface of a planet and outer space

axis (AK-sis): an imaginary line through the middle of an object, around which that object spins

galaxy (GAL-uhk-see): a very large group of stars and planets, such as the Milky Way; there are many galaxies in the universe

moon (moon): the natural satellite that orbits around Earth once each month and is visible because it reflects light from the Sun

orbit (OR-bit): the curved path followed by a moon, planet, or satellite as it circles a planet or a star like our Sun

planet (PLAN-it): a large heavenly body that orbits a star; Earth is a planet orbiting the star that we call the Sun

satellites (SAT-uh-lites): objects that orbit a planet; artificial satellites are specialized spacecrafts sent into orbit by people to gather data, send and receive communication signals, and perform other tasks

solar system (SOH-lur SIS-tuhm): the gravity-bound system of the star we call the Sun and the objects that orbit it, including eight planets; there are many solar systems in the universe

terrestrial (tuh-RES-tree-uhl): made up of rocks or metals and having a hard surface

Index

gas(es) 10, 16
layer(s) 16, 17, 18, 19
life 6, 8, 17
Milky Way 6
moon 12
people 6, 18
water 4, 5
year 14

After Reading Questions

1. How much of Earth is covered by water and what is the importance of having water on Earth?
2. What is unique about Earth's axis and why is it important?
3. What role does the Sun have in keeping life thriving on Earth?

About the Author

Kerri Mazzarella lives in south Florida with her husband, four children, and two dogs. She loves looking up at the night sky at all the stars! She lives near the Kennedy Space Center and likes to visit. Kerri enjoys learning all about planets and our solar system.

Written by: Kerri Mazzarella
Design by: Jen Bowers
Editor: Kim Thompson

Photographs/Shutterstock: cover, p. 4, 9, 16, 20 Earth ©2008 Alex Staroseltsev; cover, p.1, 8, 19 solar system ©2021 Triff; cover and interior background ©2020 Nuttawut Uttamaharad; cover Mars © Vector Tradition; p.5 ©2016 Volodimir Zozulinskyi; p.6 ©2016 Daria Grebenchuk; p.7 ©2019 Klagyivik Viktor; p.9, 18 © Vector Tradition; p.10 © Vector Tradition; p.11 ©2018 Digital Images Studio; p.12 ©2019 Brigitte Pica2; p.13 © Natee Jitthammachai; p.14 ©2017 Guenter Albers; p.15 ©2014 Anton Balazh; p.21 ©2018 aappp

Library of Congress PCN Data
Earth / Kerri Mazzarella
Our Amazing Solar System
ISBN 978-1-6389-7972-2 (hard cover)
ISBN 979-8-8873-5031-8 (paperback)
ISBN 979-8-8873-5090-5 (EPUB)
ISBN 979-8-8873-5149-0 (eBook)
Library of Congress Control Number: 2022941997

Printed in the United States of America.

Seahorse Publishing Company
www.seahorsepub.com

Published in the United States
Seahorse Publishing
PO Box 771325
Coral Springs, FL 33077